Walt Disney

www.pegasusforkids.com

© B. Jain Publishers (P) Ltd. All rights reserved. No part of this book may be reproduced, stored in a retrieval system or transmitted, in any form or by any means, mechanical, photocopying, recording or otherwise, without any prior written permission of the publisher.

Published by Kuldeep Jain for B. Jain Publishers (P) Ltd., D-157, Sector 63, Noida - 201307, U.P
Registered office: 1921/10, Chuna Mandi, Paharganj, New Delhi-110055

Printed in India

Contents

4   Who was Walt Disney?

6   Walt's Early Years

16   Walt as a Child

29   The Early Cartoons

33   Birth of Mickey Mouse and Other Cartoons

39   Post War Success

42   Disneyland—the Unique Theme Park

48   Demise of Walt: the Mastermind behind Disneyland

50   Awards, Accolades and Achievements

55   Timeline

57   Activities

60   Glossary

Who was Walt Disney?

Walt Disney was an animator, a film producer, a business tycoon, and co-founder of the Walt Disney Company. He and his brother, Roy co-founded the Walt Disney Production. He was an important figure in the 20th Century media and entertainment industry who helped to produce many films. With his immense creative genius, he created the famous cartoon characters such as Mickey Mouse and Donald Duck.

As a child, Walt Disney was very imaginative. These were his innovative thoughts in his ever active mind that won him accolades at a later stage of his life. Starting off as an ordinary animator, he eventually turned into a business tycoon. Walt Disney was a great artist who not only personified animals' characters but transformed the entertainment industry entirely with his innovative thoughts and imaginative dreams. In his four-decade long career, he transformed from being merely an animator to an artist creating masterpieces. Ultimately, he turned into a renowned personality in the entertainment business and never looked back.

The cartoon characters that people all over the world love to watch today, for instance, Mickey Mouse, Donald Duck, Goofy and Pluto are all the produce of his artistic excellence. It was his mastermind where the thought of Disneyland conceived. Apart from his contribution to the animation industry, he envisaged and laid the foundation of Disneyland. He has become immortal with the tremendous success of his Disney Theme Parks. During his lifetime, he received a record of 59 Nominations for the Academy Awards, winning 22 out of them!

Walt's Early Years

Walter Elias or 'Walt' Disney was born on December 5, 1901, in the Hermosa section of Chicago, Illinois. His father was Elias Disney, an Irish-Canadian. Flora Call Disney was his mother. She was a German-American by origin.

Walter was the fourth son of Elias Disney, a wandering carpenter, farmer, and building contractor. His mother was a school teacher. The family shifted their base to a farm near Marceline, Missouri, when Walter was still a child. It was a typical small Midwestern town. Many people think this place had served as the inspiration and model for the Main Street, U.S.A., of Disneyland. Disney was one of the five children, out of which, four were boys and one was a girl. He had three older brothers — Herbert, Raymond, and Roy and a younger sister, Ruth.

Walt lived most of his childhood in Marceline, Missouri. He had a keen interest in drawing and art. When he was seven years old, he sold small sketches and drawings to his neighbours. At the time when Walt was supposed to do his school homework, he would often doodle pictures of animals and nature. He was inspired by the scenic beauty

of the countryside surrounding his house in the farm. His flair for creating lasting art forms took shape at this time.

In 1911, his restless father abandoned his efforts at farming and moved the family to Kansas City, Missouri. There he bought a morning newspaper route and compelled

his young sons to assist him in delivering papers. Young Walt would get up at 3 o'clock every morning to deliver newspapers with his father. Once he mentioned at a later stage of his life that many of his habits and compulsions emerged from the disciplined life he had led and the discomforts he had faced while helping his father with the paper distribution .

It was here in Kansas City that young Walt began to study cartooning in a correspondence school and later took classes at the Kansas City Art Institute and School of Design.

During his childhood years, Disney developed a love for trains. His Uncle, Mike Martin, was a train engineer who worked in the route between Fort Madison, Iowa, and Marceline. Later, in the summers, Disney

worked with the railroad as a part time job. He would sell snacks, popcorn, sodas and newspapers to the travellers. Close to the Disney family farm, there were Santa Fe Railroad tracks that crossed the countryside. Often Walt would put his ear against the tracks, to listen for approaching trains. During all these years of his life, Walt would often try to recapture the freedom he felt when aboard those trains, by building his own miniature train set.

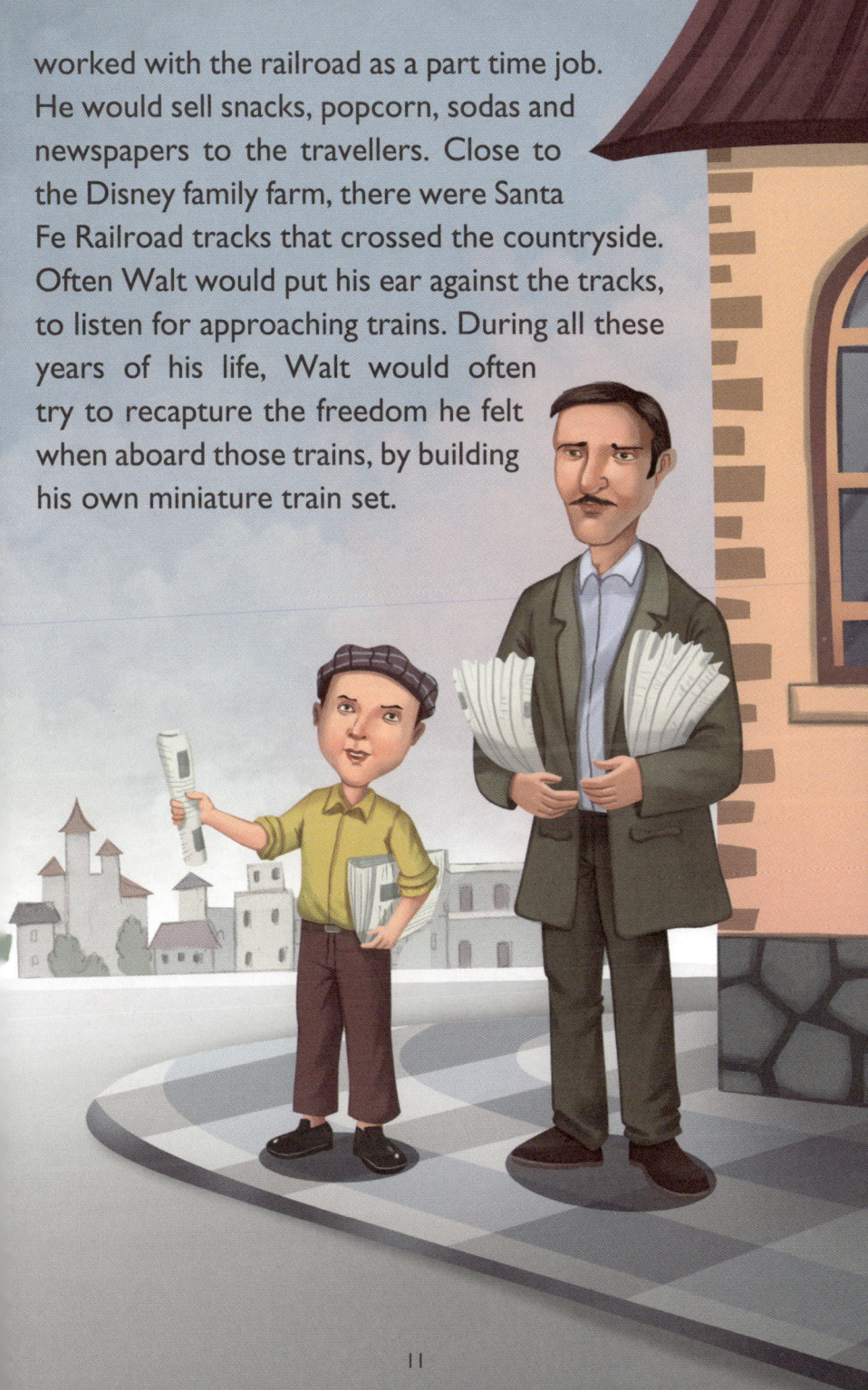

In 1917, the family moved to Chicago. Disney attended McKinley High School in Chicago where he took drawing and photography classes. He also became a contributing cartoonist for the school paper . At night, he took courses at the Chicago Art Institute to polish his drawing abilities.

Walt's love and appreciation towards nature, wildlife, family and community grew during the 'carefree years' of his life which were a large part of country life. Though his father would be quite stern and often there would be little money, Walt was encouraged by his mother and his older brother, Roy.

Though the Disney family moved to Kansas City after a while, Walt never stopped and prospered as an artist. Besides drawing, Walt had picked up a knack for acting and performing arts. At school, he began to entertain his friends by imitating his silent screen hero, Charlie Chaplin. His teachers would often invite him to tell stories to his classmates while illustrating with chalk on the board. Though his father was against many things he did, he continued pursuing his interests. He would often creep

out of his house at night in order to perform comical skits at local theaters.

During the fall of 1918, when Walt was 16 years of age, he attempted to enlist for military service. He was at once rejected because he was under age; only sixteen years old at the time. Instead, Walt joined the Red Cross and was sent overseas to France where he spent a year driving an ambulance and chauffeuring Red Cross officials. His ambulance was covered not with the usual camouflage, but with Disney cartoons!

Walt as a Child

Walt Disney's teenage was unconventional. His adolescent years were ruled by an increasingly cruel and outrageous father who was insensitive and lacked love and affection. He used to give 'corrective' beatings that became a part of their daily routine. At the slightest annoyance, Elias Disney would march them to the woodshed and give them brutal punishments. Elias's rigid self-righteousness and extreme conservatism was mirrored in the strict moral atmosphere of Kansas City during the years the Disneys lived there, i.e. 1910-17.

As Walt's childhood was mostly spent in the farms, young Walt was enchanted by it and especially its animals, both wild and domesticated, by the local railroad, and by the town of Marceline.

It is thought that Disney embraced the animals around the farm because of lack of

companionship in his family . His conservative father never allowed his sons toys and to make friends. Roy was much older and too busy working on the farm. Their mother Flora, exhausted by the household chores and broken spirit by her despotic husband, had no time for her young son.

Walt always treated pigs and other creatures as his real friends as he never had any friend throughout his childhood. Walt never learned to play the games of a boy as his father did not allow him to make friends and play with them. His

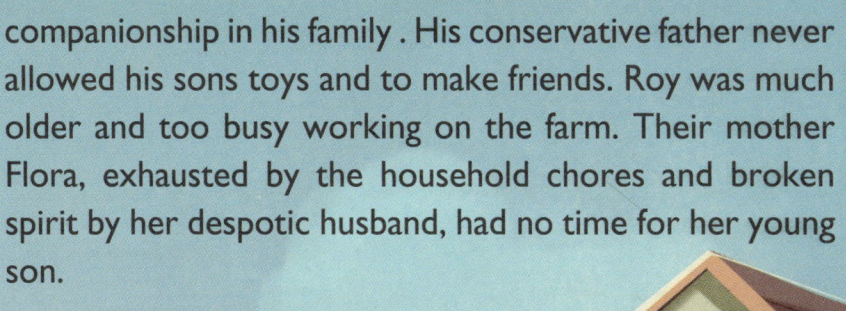

'best friend' was probably Porker, the sow. Walt later remembered in the later years, 'I guess I really loved that pig. . . . She had an acute sense of fun and mischief. Do you remember the Foolish Pig in Three Little Pigs? Porker was the model for him.'

Although Walt later romanticized this period of his childhood, it was actually a period of unkindness and loneliness for young Walt.

In the early twentieth century, where the social foundations and ethical values were constantly changing, Walt's father's outlook towards societal changes and norms were growing more and more conservative. He even encouraged certain self-destructive tendencies. Walt

came to believe that his father had been deceived in his various business ventures by other men. Elias's hidebound moralism led him not to use fertilizer on his crops. Since putting fertilizer on plants was like putting whiskey in a man!

Elias's severe attitudes gave rise to a child-rearing philosophy of 'spare the rod and spoil the child.'

Walt's encounter with his father's rigid moral and political principles brought forth an exceedingly uncertain reaction. Walt was confused. Brimming with affection and hatred

in equivalent proportions, excited both to please and to escape Elias, little sensitive Walt built up an insecurity. In almost a literal sense, it haunted him. His nightmare of forgetting to deliver some of the newspapers on his Kansas City route, his dad would 'be waiting up at that corner' to punish him for carelessness, became a part of his life.

At a later stage of life, Ward Kimball, a Disney Studio animator and a dear friend of Walt, felt that his boss could never forget his father's sternness, which in Kimball's view, adversely 'impacted Walt's friendship with other individuals'.

Walt's differences with his father and a strong disapproval of his world full of strict discipline occupied his mind and surfaced frequently even when he grew up. Throughout his life, he was eager to discuss his father. On one hand, his comments were filled with affection and admiration for the old man's virtues — the commitment to his family's welfare, the gritty work ethic, the respect for education and good citizenship. On the other hand, however,

resentment of the elder Disney's dominating behaviour would bubble out with a little push.

Walt often recollected how his father compelled him to learn the fiddle so that he would be able to make extra money as a musician. Walt neither had knack nor talent for it; he had a tough time with it and would find it difficult to hold with his right arm in the correct position. However, his father was adamant and he would often slap him firmly to make his elbow down.

When Walt helped with the carpentry as the family added space to their house, Elias frequently exploded in anger. Walt recalled this episode some forty years later. He said, "My dad was an impatient person. But he knew what he wanted to do and expected you to know just what he wanted to do . . . [and if I faltered] he'd get mad, you see. And he'd start after me. And my dad was the kind of guy who'd pick up anything near him . . . He'd pick up a saw and try to hit you with the broad side of the saw. He'd pick up a hammer, you know, and hit you with the handle."

Walt's elder sibling Roy Disney was eight years older to him. He was Walt's confidant and mentor. Walt would often snuggle cosily to him . He would often wonder if the man who beat them and give brutal punishments to them

could really be their father and why their mom never interfered and voiced against his cruelty.

'When we were kids,' Disney told one of his associates many years later, 'Roy and I slept in the same bed. I used to wet the bed and I've been pissing up Roy's leg ever since.'

Sometimes, during the day, Walt would creep into his mother's room and wore her clothes and put her makeup on. Then he would closely observe himself in the mirror. He would do that to see if he resembled his mother.

Walt experienced genuine disappointment during his Red Cross duty. When they got down in France, the contingent of young ambulance drivers were told about the danger of picking up various diseases.

In short, it may be said that Walt's childhood happenings which shaped up his future years inspired him to be what he became!

The Early Cartoons

When Walt came back from France in 1919, he shifted to Kansas City to follow his dreams which was to make a career as a newspaper artist. His brother Roy got him a job at the Pesmen-Rubin Art Studio where he met

cartoonist Ubbe Eert Iwerks, better known as Ub Iwerks. From there, Disney worked at the Kansas City Film Ad Company where he made commercials based on cutout animation. Around this time, Disney began experimenting with a camera, doing hand-drawn cel animation, and decided to open his own animation business. From the ad company, he recruited Fred Harman as his first employee.

Walt and Harman wanted to arrange the screening of their cartoons, so they made a pact with Kansas City theatre which was close by. The cartoons which were shown in the theatre became a huge hit amongst children and that made Disney buy his own studio with the same name. Laugh-O-Gram appointed several employees along with

Harman's brother Hugh and Iwerks. They made a series of seven-minute fairy tales which were a combination of both live action and animation. It was called Alice in Cartoonland. However, by 1923, the studio was weighed down with debt and Disney was forced to declare himself bankrupt.

To recover from this wretched condition, Disney and his brother, Roy, soon pooled their money and moved to Hollywood. Iwerks also relocated to California, and there the three began the Disney Brothers' Studio. Their first deal was with New York distributor Margaret Winkler, to distribute their Alice cartoons. They also invented a character called Oswald the Lucky Rabbit, and contracted the shorts at $1,500 each.

In 1925, Disney hired an ink-and-paint artist named Lillian Bounds. After a brief courtship, the couple married . Lillian gave birth to their daughter, Diane Marie Disney in 1933. They adopted Sharon Mae Disney in 1936.

Birth of Mickey Mouse and Other Cartoons

A few years later, Walt discovered to his utter shock that Winkler and her husband, Charles Mintz, had stolen the rights of Oswald, along with all of Disney's animators, except for Iwerks. Right away the Disney brothers, their wives and Iwerks produced three cartoons featuring a

new character which Walt had been developing. It was the world famous Mickey Mouse. The first animated shorts featuring Mickey were Plane Crazy and The Gallopin' Gaucho; both silent films were produced for which they could not find distributors. When sound was added into the

film, Disney created a third sound-and-music-equipped short called Steamboat Willie. This cartoon was loved by children so much that it became an instant sensation with Walt as the voice of Mickey and took the entertainment industry by storm.

There is an interesting story behind the creation of the legendary Mickey Mouse. When Walt was a child, he had mice as his pets in his farm. Moreover, he also had mice in his studios where he worked. Mice would run naughtily all around the garbage bin. Seeing those mice all his life,

Walt got inspired to make a funny and naughty mouse character along with his friends.

In 1929, Disney created Silly Symphonies, which featured Mickey's newly created friends like Minnie Mouse, Donald Duck, Goofy and Pluto. One of the most popular cartoons, Flowers and Trees, was the first to be produced in colour and to win an Oscar. In 1933, The Three Little Pigs and its title song, 'Who's Afraid of the Big Bad Wolf?' became a theme for the country in the midst of the Great Depression in America.

On December 21, 1937, Snow White and the Seven Dwarfs, the first full-length animated film, premiered in Los Angeles. It produced an unimaginable $1.499 million, in spite of the Depression, and won a total of eight Oscars! During the next five years, Walt Disney Studios completed another string of full-length animated films, Pinocchio, Fantasia, Dumbo and Bambi.

In December 1939, a new campus for Walt Disney Studios was inaugurated in Burbank. However, in 1941, its progress got hindered when the Disney animators went on a strike. Many of them resigned, and it was years before the company fully recovered. During the mid 40s, Disney created 'packaged features', groups of shorts strung together to run at feature length, but by 1950, he once again started focusing on animated features.

Post War Success

During the Second World War, there was much less demand for cartoon animation. It took until the late 1940s for Disney to recover some of his success. By 1950, when the financial condition of Walt Disney studio was alleviated, Walt focused again on feature films.

Walt finished production of Cinderella and also Peter Pan (which had been shelved during the war). In the 1950s, Walt Disney Productions also began expanding its

operations into conventional action films. They produced several successful films such as Treasure Island (1950), 20,000 Leagues Under the Sea (1954) and Pollyanna (1960).

Several animated films were released one after the other. Cinderella was released in 1950, followed by Alice in Wonderland (1951), Peter Pan (1953), a live-action film called Treasure Island (1950), Lady and the Tramp (1955), Sleeping Beauty (1959) and 101 Dalmatians (1961). In all, more than 100 features were produced by his studio.

Walt Disney was amongst the first users of television as a medium of entertainment. The Zorro and Davy Crockett series became an instant hit with children, as was The Mickey Mouse Club, a variety show featuring a cast of teenagers known as the Mouseketeers. Walt Disney used the Wonderful World of Colour, a popular Sunday night show, to promote his new theme park. The Walt Disney studio also innovated the first specifically children's shows – The Mickey Mouse Club.

In 1964, Disney's last major success that he produced himself was the motion picture's, Mary Poppins, which mixed live action and animation.

Disneyland—the Unique Theme Park

In the late 1940s, Walt Disney began building up plans for a massive theme park. Once he visited Children's fairyland in Oakland which gave him the much needed encouragement and notion of Disneyland. After investing five years in immense planning,

projecting, fund raising and execution, Disneyland Theme Park was inaugurated on July 17, 1955. The park was huge and had magnificent layout and structure. The park primarily gave the children and families an opportunity to explore the world of their imagination and fantasy. Walt Disney wished the Theme Park to be like nothing ever created on Earth. In particular, he wished it to be a magical world for children and surrounded by a train. Disney had a great love of trains since his childhood when he regularly saw trains pass near his home . It was characteristic of Walt Disney that he was willing to take risks in trying something new.

In his words Walt said, 'Courage is the main quality of leadership, in my opinion, no matter where it is exercised. Usually it implies some risk especially in new undertakings. Courage to initiate something and to keep it going, pioneering and adventurous spirit to blaze new ways, often, in our land of opportunity.'

Disneyland costed Disney brothers a whopping $17 million. The actor and future U.S. President Ronald Reagan was in charge of all the activities. After a chaotic opening day which involved several disasters, the park earned a huge recognition and became a renowned place where children and their families could explore, take rides and meet the Disney characters.

Walt's ecstasy on the opening of this unique park was clear with his opening speech when he addressed his audience when he said, 'To all who come to this happy place, welcome. Disneyland is your land. Here age relives fond memories of the past …. and here youth may savor the challenge and promise of the future. Disneyland is dedicated to the ideals, the dreams and the hard facts that have created America … with the hope that it will be a source of joy and inspiration to all the world.'

The Disneyland amusement park expanded its investment ten times, in a very brief timeframe. It was entertaining tourists from around the globe. The success and achievement that Disneyland had earned inspired Walt to consider the creation of another park in Orlando, Florida. In 1965, Walt declared another amusement park.

With the original site having some attendance ups and downs over the years, Disneyland has expanded its rides over time and branched out globally with parks in Tokyo, Paris and Hong Kong, with a Shanghai location due to open in December 2015.

Demise of Walt: the Mastermind behind Disneyland

Within a few years of opening of Disneyland, Walt started planning for another amusement park and Experimental Prototype Community of Tomorrow in Florida. It was still under construction when, in 1966, Disney was diagnosed with lung cancer. He died on December 15, 1966, at the age of 65. Disney was cremated and his body was laid in peace at the Forest Lawn Cemetery in Los Angeles, California. After his brother's death, Roy carried on the

plans to finish the Florida theme park which opened in 1971 under the name Walt Disney World.

After his demise, Walt's elder brother Roy came back to lead the Disney Company, yet the organization missed the direction, mastermind and excellence of Walt Disney. The 1970s were comparatively unproductive period for the company, before a new start in the 1980s, with a new generation of films, such as Who Framed Roger Rabbit (1988) and The Lion King (1994).

Awards, Accolades and Achievements

Walt Disney has a record of winning the most reputed Academy Awards with 22 accolades in various categories. Moreover, he was honoured with three Oscars and an

Irving Thalberg Memorial Award. Moreover, he earned a total of fifty-nine nominations. He also holds the records for most wins and most nominations of an individual in history!

Walt won his first competitive Academy Award and received his first Honorary Academy Award at the 5th Academy Awards in 1932. He received the Honorary Academy Award for the creation of Mickey Mouse and won the Academy Award for Best Short Subject (Cartoon) for the film Flowers and Trees. In the seven

Academy Award ceremonies that followed (6th–12th), Disney consecutively earned nominations and won in the same category.

Disney received three more Honorary Academy Awards. At the 26th Academy Awards in the year 1954, Disney won the Academy Award in all four categories in which he was nominated.

When Walt Disney was in his teens, he was a member of the Order of Demolay, a youth organization associated with Free Masons.

He was recognised as the father of the Tomorrowland Transit Authority in film clips showcased within the queue space of Rocket Rods (formerly, the CircleVision 360 Theater) at Disneyland.

As a young boy, he took interest particularly in personifying animals' characters after unconsciously killing a small owl. He felt guilty after this incident and repented for his act, so he pledged never to kill an innocent living creature again.

Walt was honoured with prestigious Emmy Awards also. He won total seven accolades.

In the animated short film Mickey's Rival (1936), a character named Mortimer Mouse was designed after him.

Walt shortlisted Anaheim, California as the prime location for Disneyland. The demographics experts convinced him saying that it would be a major centre of attraction for people within 10 years. They were absolutely right as the rest is history.

Timeline

- 1901 Walt Disney was born on the 5th of December
- 1910 the Disney family moved to Kansas City
- 1917 Walt's family migrated to Chicago; Walt joined the Red Cross
- 1920 Walt returned from France; when he got to the states, Ub Iwerks and he soon open the cartoon company Laugh-O-Grams.
- 1923 after Laugh-O-Grams went bankrupt, Walt went to Hollywood and he and his brother Roy, opened a cartoon company.
- 1927 Walt's studio started creating a series of Oswald the Lucky Rabbit cartoons but soon lost all rights to Oswald to Mitz company
- 1928 Mickey Mouse was created; the cartoons Plane Crazy and Steamboat Willie followed
- 1932 Flowers and Trees, a Silly Symphonies cartoon done in Technicolor, won the Academy Award for Best Short Subject: Cartoons.
- 1933 the cartoon called The Three Little Pigs became a big success

Timeline

- **1934** in the cartoon, Orphan's Benefit, Donald Duck was introduced into the Mickey Mouse world

- **1938** Snow White was released; the film was a huge success and earned an amount of $8 million

- **1940** During the late 1940s, Disney continued the work on Alice in Wonderland and Peter Pan and started work on Cinderella. He had been to Chicago in the late 1940s. There he sketched his ideas for an amusement park, deriving inspiration from the Children's Fairyland in Oakland, California. This later gave way to the creation of Disneyland!

- **1950** Treasure Island and 20,000 Leagues Under the Sea were produced

- **1955** on September 8, 1955, Disneyland was proud to welcome its one-millionth visitor! Mickey Mouse Club became the first daily television show

- **1964** Mary Poppins became the most popular Disney film of the 1960s. It received nominations for 13 academic awards

- **1966** on November 30, Disney was admitted to St. Joseph's Hospital. On December 15, Walt Disney died of lung cancer

Class Discussion

Do you watch cartoons? If yes, which ones are your favourite and why? Share in the class with your teacher and friends.

Pair and Share

You and your partner get together. Make a collage with pictures of any one of your favourite cartoon character. Both of you should bring equal number of pictures. Do bring a glue stick, 2 pairs of scissors and colours.

Note: Do tell your teacher which cartoon characters you have chosen.

Have you been to a theme park? Collect pictures and information about Disneyland.

Question

1. Who was Walt Disney?
2. What comes to your mind when you hear this name?
3. When and where was Disney born?
4. Do you remember the names of his parents?

Activities

5. What did his father and mother do for living?

6. How many brothers and sisters did Walt have? Do you remember their names?

7. When Walt was a young child, what did he like to do the most?

8. Name the institute where he took classes in Kansas City?

9. Walt loved trains. What did he do to earn money on trains?

10. Can you name the school that Walt went to in Chicago?

11. Describe in brief the relation Walt shared with his father Elias Disney?

12. Do you think that affected him in his later life?

13. do you think Walt's love for animals affected his work?

14. Name the cartoon character Walt had first created and which was stolen?

15. How did he get the idea of creating Mickey Mouse?

16. Name the cartoonist who was a partner in Walt's work.

17. Which quality did Walt think was important in a leader? Do you think he himself had that?

18. Name the first studio that Walt owned?

19. When and how was Disneyland opened?

20. What was Walt's idea behind opening it?

21. Was Disneyland a success or a failure?

22. When and how did Walt Disney die

Glossary

abandoned: to be deserted or left by someone

Academy Awards: The Academy Awards or The Oscars is an annual American awards ceremony to honour cinematic achievements in the film industry

agrarian: anything related to cultivated land or the cultivation

amusement: entertainment or enjoyment

animation: the technique of photographing successive drawings or positions of puppets or models to create an illusion of movement

animators: a person who makes animated films

appreciation: recognition of the full worth of someone or something

brutal: Savagely violent

carelessness: not to give sufficient attention to something

cartoonist: an artist who draws cartoons

category: a class or division of people or things regarded as having the same characteristics

chaotic: disordered or in a state of complete confusion

chores: routine tasks that occur in a household

Glossary

compulsions: an irresistible wish to behave in a certain way

conservatism: to believe in old values; not modern

contractor: a person or firm that undertakes a contract to provide materials or labour

conventional: a person who is greatly concerned with what is socially acceptable

cremated: a funeral ceremony in which a dead person's body is disposed of by burnig it to ashes

declared: announced

despotic: a person who exerts his power forcefully

diagnosed: to identify the nature of an illness

disagreement: lack of approval

discomforts: to make someone feel anxious or embarrassed

distribution: to share something amongst many

dominating: to have power to influence over others

doodle: to make a drawing carelessly

enchanted: to fill someone with great delight

Glossary

entertainment: to provide someone with amusement or enjoyment

episode: an event or a group of events occurring in sequence

execution: completing or carrying out something

exhausted: to be very tired

expanded: extended or stretched

features: a distinctive aspect of something

fiddle: a violin

garbage: waste products

Great Depression: was a severe worldwide economic depression in the decade preceding World War II. In most countries it started in 1930 and lasted until the late 1930s or middle 1940s.

hidebound: unable to change because of tradition or convention

honorary: to confer as an honour without the usual requirements

imitating: to follow someone's styles or actions

immense: huge or vast in amount

immortal: living forever, not dying

insecurity: the state of being uncertain about oneself; lack of protection or confidence

Glossary

inspired: encouraged or motivated

interfered: to get in the way of something or somebody

invented: to create or design something new

investment: the process of putting or funding money for profit

magnificent: wonderful or extremely beautiful

moralism: the habit of making judgements about others' morality

nominations: the action of nominating someone for their performance

notion: idea

popular: liked or admired by many people

production: the act of making or manufacturing something from raw materials

recapture: to capture again

recruited: to enlist someone in a company for a job

rejected: to dismiss

self-righteousness: to be moral; not doing wrong

sensation: a physical feeling resulting from something

Glossary

theme parks: an amusement park with a similar setting all over

tremendous: in very great amount

tycoon: a wealthy, powerful person in business or industry

unique: only one of its kind

wretched: of poor quality